50 Homemade Ice Cream Flavors

By: Kelly Johnson

Table of Contents

- Vanilla Bean
- Classic Chocolate
- Strawberry Delight
- Mint Chocolate Chip
- Cookies and Cream
- Rocky Road
- Salted Caramel
- Butter Pecan
- Espresso Coffee
- Honey Lavender
- Matcha Green Tea
- Pistachio Bliss
- Mango Sorbet
- Lemon Basil
- Blackberry Cheesecake
- Peanut Butter Swirl
- Maple Walnut
- Dark Chocolate Raspberry
- Coconut Cream
- Blueberry Pie
- Chai Spice
- White Chocolate Peppermint
- Almond Joy
- Dulce de Leche
- Chocolate Fudge Brownie
- Cherry Garcia
- Key Lime Pie
- Banana Pudding
- Cinnamon Roll
- Nutella Hazelnut
- Carrot Cake
- Mocha Chip
- Red Velvet
- S'mores Delight
- Watermelon Sorbet

- Honey Roasted Almond
- Gingerbread Cookie
- Chocolate Orange
- Pomegranate Berry
- Sweet Corn
- Earl Grey Tea
- Pumpkin Spice
- Black Sesame
- Taro Coconut
- Huckleberry Bliss
- Brown Sugar Bourbon
- Candy Cane Crunch
- Fig and Honey
- Chocolate Chili
- Lavender Blueberry

Vanilla Bean Ice Cream

Ingredients:

- 2 cups heavy cream
- 1 cup whole milk
- 3/4 cup granulated sugar
- 1 vanilla bean (or 2 tsp pure vanilla extract)
- 4 large egg yolks

Instructions:

1. **Prepare the Vanilla:** Slice the vanilla bean lengthwise and scrape out the seeds. Add both the seeds and pod to a saucepan with the heavy cream, milk, and half of the sugar. Heat over medium heat until steaming (do not boil). Remove from heat and let it steep for 15 minutes.
2. **Whisk the Egg Yolks:** In a separate bowl, whisk the egg yolks with the remaining sugar until pale and creamy.
3. **Temper the Eggs:** Slowly pour the warm cream mixture into the egg yolks while whisking constantly. Return the mixture to the saucepan.
4. **Cook the Custard:** Cook over low heat, stirring constantly, until the mixture thickens and coats the back of a spoon (about 170–175°F or 77–80°C). Do not let it boil.
5. **Strain & Chill:** Remove from heat and strain through a fine-mesh sieve into a bowl. Discard the vanilla pod. Cover and chill for at least 4 hours or overnight.
6. **Churn the Ice Cream:** Pour the chilled custard into an ice cream maker and churn according to the manufacturer's instructions.
7. **Freeze & Serve:** Transfer to an airtight container and freeze for at least 2 hours before serving.

Classic Chocolate Ice Cream

Ingredients:

- 2 cups heavy cream
- 1 cup whole milk
- 3/4 cup granulated sugar
- 1/2 cup unsweetened cocoa powder
- 4 large egg yolks
- 4 oz dark chocolate, melted
- 1 tsp pure vanilla extract

Instructions:

1. Heat cream, milk, sugar, and cocoa powder in a saucepan over medium heat until steaming (do not boil).
2. Whisk egg yolks in a separate bowl. Slowly add warm mixture while whisking constantly.
3. Return to saucepan and cook over low heat until thickened (170–175°F). Stir in melted chocolate and vanilla.
4. Strain and chill for at least 4 hours.
5. Churn in an ice cream maker, then freeze for 2+ hours.

Strawberry Delight Ice Cream

Ingredients:

- 2 cups fresh strawberries, hulled and chopped
- 3/4 cup granulated sugar
- 2 cups heavy cream
- 1 cup whole milk
- 1 tsp lemon juice
- 1 tsp pure vanilla extract

Instructions:

1. Mash strawberries with 1/4 cup sugar and lemon juice; let sit for 15 minutes.
2. Heat cream, milk, and remaining sugar over medium heat until steaming.
3. Stir in vanilla and chilled strawberries.
4. Chill for at least 4 hours, then churn in an ice cream maker.
5. Freeze for 2+ hours before serving.

Mint Chocolate Chip Ice Cream

Ingredients:

- 2 cups heavy cream
- 1 cup whole milk
- 3/4 cup granulated sugar
- 1 tsp pure peppermint extract
- 4 large egg yolks
- 4 oz semisweet chocolate, finely chopped
- Optional: Green food coloring

Instructions:

1. Heat cream, milk, and sugar over medium heat until steaming.
2. Whisk egg yolks separately, then slowly mix in warm milk.
3. Cook over low heat until thickened (170–175°F), then stir in peppermint extract.
4. Chill for at least 4 hours.
5. Churn in an ice cream maker. Fold in chocolate before freezing for 2+ hours.

Cookies and Cream Ice Cream

Ingredients:

- 2 cups heavy cream
- 1 cup whole milk
- 3/4 cup granulated sugar
- 1 tsp pure vanilla extract
- 10–12 chocolate sandwich cookies, crushed

Instructions:

1. Heat cream, milk, and sugar over medium heat until steaming. Remove from heat and stir in vanilla.
2. Chill for at least 4 hours.
3. Churn in an ice cream maker. Fold in crushed cookies before freezing for 2+ hours.

Rocky Road Ice Cream

Ingredients:

- 2 cups heavy cream
- 1 cup whole milk
- 3/4 cup granulated sugar
- 1/2 cup unsweetened cocoa powder
- 4 oz dark chocolate, melted
- 1 tsp vanilla extract
- 1 cup mini marshmallows
- 1/2 cup chopped toasted almonds

Instructions:

1. Heat cream, milk, sugar, and cocoa powder over medium heat until steaming.
2. Whisk egg yolks in a bowl, temper with warm mixture, and return to saucepan. Cook until thickened (170–175°F).
3. Stir in melted chocolate and vanilla. Chill for 4+ hours.
4. Churn, then fold in marshmallows and almonds before freezing for 2+ hours.

Salted Caramel Ice Cream

Ingredients:

- 1 cup granulated sugar
- 2 cups heavy cream
- 1 cup whole milk
- 4 large egg yolks
- 1 tsp vanilla extract
- 1/2 tsp sea salt

Instructions:

1. Melt sugar in a saucepan over medium heat until amber-colored. Carefully whisk in cream.
2. Add milk and heat until steaming. Whisk egg yolks separately, temper with warm mixture, and return to saucepan.
3. Cook until thickened, then stir in vanilla and salt.
4. Chill, churn, and freeze for 2+ hours.

Butter Pecan Ice Cream

Ingredients:

- 1 cup pecans, chopped
- 2 tbsp butter
- 2 cups heavy cream
- 1 cup whole milk
- 3/4 cup granulated sugar
- 4 large egg yolks
- 1 tsp vanilla extract

Instructions:

1. Toast pecans in butter for 3 minutes; set aside.
2. Heat cream, milk, and sugar until steaming. Whisk egg yolks separately, temper, and cook until thickened.
3. Stir in vanilla, chill for 4+ hours, then churn.
4. Fold in pecans before freezing for 2+ hours.

Espresso Coffee Ice Cream

Ingredients:

- 2 cups heavy cream
- 1 cup whole milk
- 3/4 cup granulated sugar
- 2 tbsp instant espresso powder
- 4 large egg yolks
- 1 tsp vanilla extract

Instructions:

1. Heat cream, milk, sugar, and espresso powder over medium heat until steaming.
2. Whisk egg yolks separately, temper, and return to saucepan. Cook until thickened.
3. Stir in vanilla, chill, churn, and freeze for 2+ hours.

Honey Lavender Ice Cream

Ingredients:

- 2 cups heavy cream
- 1 cup whole milk
- 3/4 cup honey
- 2 tbsp dried culinary lavender
- 4 large egg yolks

Instructions:

1. Heat cream, milk, honey, and lavender until steaming. Let steep for 15 minutes, then strain.
2. Whisk egg yolks separately, temper, and cook until thickened.
3. Chill, churn, and freeze for 2+ hours.

Matcha Green Tea Ice Cream

Ingredients:

- 2 cups heavy cream
- 1 cup whole milk
- 3/4 cup granulated sugar
- 2 tbsp matcha powder
- 4 large egg yolks

Instructions:

1. Heat cream, milk, sugar, and matcha until steaming.
2. Whisk egg yolks separately, temper, and cook until thickened.
3. Chill, churn, and freeze for 2+ hours.

Pistachio Bliss Ice Cream

Ingredients:

- 1 cup shelled unsalted pistachios
- 2 cups heavy cream
- 1 cup whole milk
- 3/4 cup granulated sugar
- 4 large egg yolks
- 1/2 tsp almond extract

Instructions:

1. Blend pistachios with 1/2 cup milk until smooth.
2. Heat cream, milk, sugar, and pistachio mixture until steaming.
3. Whisk egg yolks separately, temper, and cook until thickened.
4. Stir in almond extract, chill, churn, and freeze for 2+ hours.

Mango Sorbet

Ingredients:

- 3 ripe mangoes, peeled and chopped
- 3/4 cup sugar
- 1/2 cup water
- 1 tbsp lime juice

Instructions:

1. Blend all ingredients until smooth.
2. Chill for 2+ hours, then churn in an ice cream maker.
3. Freeze for 2+ hours before serving.

Lemon Basil Ice Cream

Ingredients:

- 2 cups heavy cream
- 1 cup whole milk
- 3/4 cup sugar
- Zest of 1 lemon
- 2 tbsp chopped fresh basil
- 4 large egg yolks

Instructions:

1. Heat cream, milk, sugar, lemon zest, and basil until steaming. Let steep for 15 minutes, then strain.
2. Whisk egg yolks separately, temper, and cook until thickened.
3. Chill, churn, and freeze for 2+ hours.

Blackberry Cheesecake Ice Cream

Ingredients:

- 2 cups heavy cream
- 1 cup whole milk
- 8 oz cream cheese, softened
- 3/4 cup sugar
- 1 cup fresh blackberries, mashed
- 1 tsp vanilla extract
- 1/2 cup graham cracker crumbs

Instructions:

1. Blend cream cheese, sugar, and vanilla until smooth.
2. Heat cream and milk until steaming, then mix into cream cheese mixture.
3. Chill for 4+ hours, then churn.
4. Fold in blackberries and graham crackers before freezing for 2+ hours.

Peanut Butter Swirl Ice Cream

Ingredients:

- 2 cups heavy cream
- 1 cup whole milk
- 3/4 cup sugar
- 1 tsp vanilla extract
- 1/2 cup creamy peanut butter

Instructions:

1. Heat cream, milk, and sugar until steaming. Stir in vanilla.
2. Chill for 4+ hours, then churn.
3. Swirl in peanut butter before freezing for 2+ hours.

Maple Walnut Ice Cream

Ingredients:

- 2 cups heavy cream
- 1 cup whole milk
- 3/4 cup pure maple syrup
- 4 large egg yolks
- 1 tsp vanilla extract
- 3/4 cup chopped toasted walnuts

Instructions:

1. Heat cream, milk, and maple syrup until steaming.
2. Whisk egg yolks separately, temper, and cook until thickened.
3. Stir in vanilla, chill, churn, and fold in walnuts before freezing for 2+ hours.

Dark Chocolate Raspberry Ice Cream

Ingredients:

- 2 cups heavy cream
- 1 cup whole milk
- 3/4 cup sugar
- 1/2 cup unsweetened cocoa powder
- 4 oz dark chocolate, melted
- 1 tsp vanilla extract
- 1 cup fresh raspberries

Instructions:

1. Heat cream, milk, sugar, and cocoa powder until steaming.
2. Whisk egg yolks separately, temper, and cook until thickened. Stir in melted chocolate and vanilla.
3. Chill for 4+ hours, then churn.
4. Fold in raspberries before freezing for 2+ hours.

Coconut Cream Ice Cream

Ingredients:

- 1 can (13.5 oz) coconut milk
- 1 cup heavy cream
- 3/4 cup sugar
- 1 tsp vanilla extract
- 1/2 cup toasted coconut flakes

Instructions:

1. Heat coconut milk, cream, and sugar until steaming. Stir in vanilla.
2. Chill for 4+ hours, then churn.
3. Fold in toasted coconut before freezing for 2+ hours.

Blueberry Pie Ice Cream

Ingredients:

- 2 cups heavy cream
- 1 cup whole milk
- 3/4 cup sugar
- 1 tsp vanilla extract
- 1 cup fresh blueberries, mashed
- 1/2 cup crumbled pie crust

Instructions:

1. Heat cream, milk, and sugar until steaming. Stir in vanilla.
2. Chill for 4+ hours, then churn.
3. Fold in blueberries and pie crust before freezing for 2+ hours.

Chai Spice Ice Cream

Ingredients:

- 2 cups heavy cream
- 1 cup whole milk
- 3/4 cup sugar
- 2 chai tea bags
- 1 tsp vanilla extract
- 1/2 tsp cinnamon
- 1/4 tsp ground ginger
- 1/4 tsp cardamom

Instructions:

1. Heat cream, milk, sugar, and chai tea bags until steaming. Let steep for 15 minutes, then remove tea bags.
2. Stir in vanilla and spices, then chill for 4+ hours.
3. Churn and freeze for 2+ hours.

White Chocolate Peppermint Ice Cream

Ingredients:

- 2 cups heavy cream
- 1 cup whole milk
- 3/4 cup sugar
- 4 oz white chocolate, melted
- 1/2 tsp peppermint extract
- 1/2 cup crushed peppermint candies

Instructions:

1. Heat cream, milk, and sugar until steaming. Stir in melted white chocolate and peppermint extract.
2. Chill for 4+ hours, then churn.
3. Fold in crushed candies before freezing for 2+ hours.

Almond Joy Ice Cream

Ingredients:

- 2 cups heavy cream
- 1 cup coconut milk
- 3/4 cup sugar
- 1 tsp vanilla extract
- 1/2 cup toasted coconut flakes
- 1/2 cup chopped almonds
- 1/2 cup chocolate chips

Instructions:

1. Heat cream, coconut milk, and sugar until steaming. Stir in vanilla.
2. Chill for 4+ hours, then churn.
3. Fold in coconut, almonds, and chocolate before freezing for 2+ hours.

Dulce de Leche Ice Cream

Ingredients:

- 1 can (14 oz) dulce de leche
- 2 cups heavy cream
- 1 cup whole milk
- 1/2 tsp sea salt
- 1 tsp vanilla extract

Instructions:

1. Heat dulce de leche, cream, milk, and salt until steaming. Stir in vanilla.
2. Chill for 4+ hours, then churn.
3. Freeze for 2+ hours before serving.

Chocolate Fudge Brownie Ice Cream

Ingredients:

- 2 cups heavy cream
- 1 cup whole milk
- 3/4 cup sugar
- 1/2 cup unsweetened cocoa powder
- 4 oz dark chocolate, melted
- 1 tsp vanilla extract
- 1 cup fudgy brownie chunks

Instructions:

1. Heat cream, milk, sugar, and cocoa powder until steaming.
2. Whisk egg yolks separately, temper, and cook until thickened (170–175°F). Stir in melted chocolate and vanilla.
3. Chill for 4+ hours, then churn.
4. Fold in brownie chunks before freezing for 2+ hours.

Cherry Garcia Ice Cream

Ingredients:

- 2 cups heavy cream
- 1 cup whole milk
- 3/4 cup sugar
- 1 tsp vanilla extract
- 1 cup fresh cherries, chopped
- 1/2 cup dark chocolate chunks

Instructions:

1. Heat cream, milk, and sugar until steaming. Stir in vanilla.
2. Chill for 4+ hours, then churn.
3. Fold in cherries and chocolate before freezing for 2+ hours.

Key Lime Pie Ice Cream

Ingredients:

- 2 cups heavy cream
- 1 cup whole milk
- 3/4 cup sugar
- Zest and juice of 3 key limes
- 1 tsp vanilla extract
- 1/2 cup crushed graham crackers

Instructions:

1. Heat cream, milk, sugar, lime zest, and juice until steaming. Stir in vanilla.
2. Chill for 4+ hours, then churn.
3. Fold in graham crackers before freezing for 2+ hours.

Banana Pudding Ice Cream

Ingredients:

- 2 ripe bananas, mashed
- 2 cups heavy cream
- 1 cup whole milk
- 3/4 cup sugar
- 1 tsp vanilla extract
- 1/2 cup crushed vanilla wafers

Instructions:

1. Blend bananas with cream, milk, sugar, and vanilla.
2. Chill for 4+ hours, then churn.
3. Fold in vanilla wafers before freezing for 2+ hours.

Cinnamon Roll Ice Cream

Ingredients:

- 2 cups heavy cream
- 1 cup whole milk
- 3/4 cup sugar
- 1 tsp vanilla extract
- 1 tsp cinnamon
- 1/2 cup cinnamon roll pieces
- 1/4 cup caramel sauce

Instructions:

1. Heat cream, milk, sugar, vanilla, and cinnamon until steaming.
2. Chill for 4+ hours, then churn.
3. Fold in cinnamon roll pieces and swirl in caramel before freezing for 2+ hours.

Nutella Hazelnut Ice Cream

Ingredients:

- 2 cups heavy cream
- 1 cup whole milk
- 3/4 cup sugar
- 1/2 cup Nutella
- 1/2 cup chopped toasted hazelnuts

Instructions:

1. Heat cream, milk, and sugar until steaming. Stir in Nutella.
2. Chill for 4+ hours, then churn.
3. Fold in hazelnuts before freezing for 2+ hours.

Carrot Cake Ice Cream

Ingredients:

- 2 cups heavy cream
- 1 cup whole milk
- 3/4 cup sugar
- 1 tsp cinnamon
- 1/2 tsp nutmeg
- 1/2 tsp vanilla extract
- 1/2 cup grated carrot
- 1/2 cup crumbled carrot cake

Instructions:

1. Heat cream, milk, sugar, cinnamon, nutmeg, and vanilla until steaming.
2. Chill for 4+ hours, then churn.
3. Fold in grated carrot and carrot cake before freezing for 2+ hours.

Mocha Chip Ice Cream

Ingredients:

- 2 cups heavy cream
- 1 cup whole milk
- 3/4 cup sugar
- 2 tbsp instant espresso powder
- 4 oz dark chocolate, chopped
- 1 tsp vanilla extract

Instructions:

1. Heat cream, milk, sugar, and espresso powder until steaming.
2. Chill for 4+ hours, then churn.
3. Fold in chocolate before freezing for 2+ hours.

Red Velvet Ice Cream

Ingredients:

- 2 cups heavy cream
- 1 cup whole milk
- 3/4 cup sugar
- 1/4 cup unsweetened cocoa powder
- 1 tsp vanilla extract
- 1/2 tsp red food coloring
- 1/2 cup crumbled red velvet cake
- 1/4 cup cream cheese, softened

Instructions:

1. Heat cream, milk, sugar, cocoa powder, and vanilla until steaming.
2. Whisk in cream cheese and food coloring until smooth.
3. Chill for 4+ hours, then churn.
4. Fold in cake crumbs before freezing for 2+ hours.

S'mores Delight Ice Cream

Ingredients:

- 2 cups heavy cream
- 1 cup whole milk
- 3/4 cup sugar
- 1 tsp vanilla extract
- 1/2 cup mini marshmallows
- 1/2 cup crumbled graham crackers
- 1/2 cup chocolate chunks

Instructions:

1. Heat cream, milk, sugar, and vanilla until steaming.
2. Chill for 4+ hours, then churn.
3. Fold in marshmallows, graham crackers, and chocolate before freezing for 2+ hours.

Watermelon Sorbet

Ingredients:

- 4 cups watermelon, cubed and seedless
- 3/4 cup sugar
- 1 tbsp lemon juice
- 1/2 cup water

Instructions:

1. Blend watermelon, sugar, lemon juice, and water until smooth.
2. Chill for 2+ hours, then churn.
3. Freeze for 2+ hours before serving.

Honey Roasted Almond Ice Cream

Ingredients:

- 2 cups heavy cream
- 1 cup whole milk
- 3/4 cup honey
- 4 large egg yolks
- 1/2 cup roasted almonds, chopped

Instructions:

1. Heat cream, milk, and honey until steaming.
2. Whisk egg yolks separately, temper, and cook until thickened.
3. Chill for 4+ hours, then churn.
4. Fold in almonds before freezing for 2+ hours.

Gingerbread Cookie Ice Cream

Ingredients:

- 2 cups heavy cream
- 1 cup whole milk
- 3/4 cup sugar
- 1 tsp cinnamon
- 1/2 tsp ground ginger
- 1/4 tsp nutmeg
- 1/2 tsp vanilla extract
- 1/2 cup crumbled gingerbread cookies

Instructions:

1. Heat cream, milk, sugar, and spices until steaming.
2. Chill for 4+ hours, then churn.
3. Fold in cookie crumbles before freezing for 2+ hours.

Chocolate Orange Ice Cream

Ingredients:

- 2 cups heavy cream
- 1 cup whole milk
- 3/4 cup sugar
- 1/2 cup unsweetened cocoa powder
- Zest of 1 orange
- 1 tsp vanilla extract
- 1/2 cup dark chocolate chunks

Instructions:

1. Heat cream, milk, sugar, cocoa powder, and orange zest until steaming.
2. Chill for 4+ hours, then churn.
3. Fold in chocolate chunks before freezing for 2+ hours.

Pomegranate Berry Ice Cream

Ingredients:

- 1 cup pomegranate juice
- 1 cup mixed berries (strawberries, raspberries, blueberries)
- 3/4 cup sugar
- 2 cups heavy cream
- 1 cup whole milk

Instructions:

1. Blend pomegranate juice, berries, and sugar until smooth.
2. Heat cream and milk until steaming, then mix with berry blend.
3. Chill for 4+ hours, then churn.
4. Freeze for 2+ hours before serving.

Sweet Corn Ice Cream

Ingredients:

- 2 cups heavy cream
- 1 cup whole milk
- 3/4 cup sugar
- 1 cup fresh sweet corn kernels
- 1 tsp vanilla extract

Instructions:

1. Heat cream, milk, sugar, and corn until steaming. Let steep for 15 minutes, then blend and strain.
2. Chill for 4+ hours, then churn.
3. Freeze for 2+ hours before serving.

Earl Grey Tea Ice Cream

Ingredients:

- 2 cups heavy cream
- 1 cup whole milk
- 3/4 cup sugar
- 2 Earl Grey tea bags
- 4 large egg yolks

Instructions:

1. Heat cream, milk, sugar, and tea bags until steaming. Let steep for 15 minutes, then remove tea bags.
2. Whisk egg yolks separately, temper, and cook until thickened.
3. Chill for 4+ hours, then churn.
4. Freeze for 2+ hours before serving.

Pumpkin Spice Ice Cream

Ingredients:

- 2 cups heavy cream
- 1 cup whole milk
- 3/4 cup brown sugar
- 3/4 cup pumpkin purée
- 1 tsp cinnamon
- 1/2 tsp nutmeg
- 1/4 tsp ginger
- 1 tsp vanilla extract

Instructions:

1. Heat cream, milk, sugar, pumpkin, and spices until steaming.
2. Chill for 4+ hours, then churn.
3. Freeze for 2+ hours before serving.

Black Sesame Ice Cream

Ingredients:

- 2 cups heavy cream
- 1 cup whole milk
- 3/4 cup sugar
- 1/2 cup black sesame seeds, toasted and ground
- 4 large egg yolks

Instructions:

1. Heat cream, milk, sugar, and black sesame paste until steaming.
2. Whisk egg yolks separately, temper, and cook until thickened.
3. Chill for 4+ hours, then churn.
4. Freeze for 2+ hours before serving.

Taro Coconut Ice Cream

Ingredients:

- 1 cup taro root, peeled and diced
- 1 can (13.5 oz) coconut milk
- 1 cup heavy cream
- 3/4 cup sugar
- 1 tsp vanilla extract

Instructions:

1. Boil taro until soft, then blend with coconut milk.
2. Heat taro mixture with cream and sugar until steaming.
3. Chill for 4+ hours, then churn.
4. Freeze for 2+ hours before serving.

Huckleberry Bliss Ice Cream

Ingredients:

- 2 cups fresh huckleberries
- 3/4 cup sugar
- 2 cups heavy cream
- 1 cup whole milk
- 1 tsp lemon juice

Instructions:

1. Mash huckleberries with sugar and lemon juice; let sit for 15 minutes.
2. Heat cream and milk until steaming, then mix with berries.
3. Chill for 4+ hours, then churn.
4. Freeze for 2+ hours before serving.

Brown Sugar Bourbon Ice Cream

Ingredients:

- 2 cups heavy cream
- 1 cup whole milk
- 3/4 cup brown sugar
- 2 tbsp bourbon
- 1 tsp vanilla extract

Instructions:

1. Heat cream, milk, and brown sugar until steaming.
2. Stir in bourbon and vanilla.
3. Chill for 4+ hours, then churn.
4. Freeze for 2+ hours before serving.

Candy Cane Crunch Ice Cream

Ingredients:

- 2 cups heavy cream
- 1 cup whole milk
- 3/4 cup sugar
- 1/2 tsp peppermint extract
- 1/2 cup crushed candy canes
- 1/2 cup white chocolate chips

Instructions:

1. Heat cream, milk, and sugar until steaming. Stir in peppermint extract.
2. Chill for 4+ hours, then churn.
3. Fold in crushed candy canes and white chocolate before freezing for 2+ hours.

Fig and Honey Ice Cream

Ingredients:

- 2 cups heavy cream
- 1 cup whole milk
- 3/4 cup honey
- 1 cup fresh figs, chopped

Instructions:

1. Heat cream, milk, and honey until steaming.
2. Chill for 4+ hours, then churn.
3. Fold in figs before freezing for 2+ hours.

Chocolate Chili Ice Cream

Ingredients:

- 2 cups heavy cream
- 1 cup whole milk
- 3/4 cup sugar
- 1/2 cup unsweetened cocoa powder
- 1/2 tsp cayenne pepper
- 1/2 tsp cinnamon
- 4 oz dark chocolate, melted

Instructions:

1. Heat cream, milk, sugar, cocoa powder, and spices until steaming.
2. Stir in melted chocolate.
3. Chill for 4+ hours, then churn.
4. Freeze for 2+ hours before serving.

Lavender Blueberry Ice Cream

Ingredients:

- 2 cups heavy cream
- 1 cup whole milk
- 3/4 cup sugar
- 1 tbsp dried culinary lavender
- 1 cup fresh blueberries, mashed

Instructions:

1. Heat cream, milk, sugar, and lavender until steaming. Let steep for 15 minutes, then strain.
2. Chill for 4+ hours, then churn.
3. Fold in blueberries before freezing for 2+ hours.

www.ingramcontent.com/pod-product-compliance
Lightning Source LLC
LaVergne TN
LVHW081339060526
838201LV00055B/2739